W9-DGF-437

A HISTORICAL ALBUM OF

PENNSYLVANIA

PENNSYLVANIA

Charles A. Wills

THE MILLBROOK PRESS, Brookfield, Connecticut

Library of Congress Cataloging-in-Publication Data

Wills, Charles A.
    A historical album of Pennsylvania / Charles A. Wills.
        p. cm. — (Historical albums)
    Includes bibliographical references and index.
    Summary: A history of Pennsylvania, from its early exploration and
settlement to the state today.
    ISBN 1-56294-595-5 (lib. bdg.)   ISBN 1-56294-853-9 (pbk.)
    1. Pennsylvania—History—Juvenile literature. 2. Pennsylvania—
Gazetteers—Juvenile literature. I. Title. II. Series.
    F149.3.W55 1996
    974.8—dc20   95-40266
                                                             CIP
                                                              AC

 Created in association with Media Projects Incorporated

    C. Carter Smith, *Executive Editor*
    Kimberly Horstman, *Project Editor*
    Charles A. Wills, *Principal Writer*
    Bernard Schleifer, *Art Director*
    John Kern, *Production Editor*
    Arlene Goldberg, *Cartographer*

    Consultant: Melissa Wisehaupt, Teacher Consultant for the Pennsylvania
    Geographic Alliance and Language Arts/Social Studies faculty member at the
    Bellefonte Area Middle School, Bellefonte, Pennsylvania

CONTENTS

Introduction

A keystone is the wedge of stone that lies in the center of an arch. In other words, it is the stone that holds all the others together. No wonder, then, that Pennsylvania is called the Keystone State. Lying in the middle of North America's Atlantic Coast, separating north from south, Pennsylvania was at the geographical center of the original thirteen colonies that became the first states.

But Pennsylvania's nickname reflects more than its place on the map. Pennsylvania is also the keystone of American history. The drafting of the Declaration of Independence, the framing of the Constitution, the Battle of Gettysburg—all of these great events took place in Pennsylvania. Pennsylvania's great natural wealth, too, made it a keystone in the nation's economic development.

Pennsylvania's unique heritage has much to do with the dream of its founder, William Penn, who established the colony more than three centuries ago. Penn created Pennsylvania not as a refuge for one group of people, like the Puritans of New England, nor as a business venture, like Virginia and other Southern colonies. Instead, Penn established Pennsylvania as a place where people of all cultures and faiths could live together in peace.

Pennsylvania has grown from a colony of a few hundred settlers to a powerful state with more than 12 million residents, but much of Penn's great vision endures. Although Pennsylvania has faced many changes and challenges since its founding, the success of Penn's "Holy Experiment" still shines as a bright spot not only in American history, but in the history of the world.

THE KEYSTONE STATE

John Rubens Smith painted this lively view of Philadelphia's busy Chestnut Street as it appeared in 1844. Founded in 1682 by William Penn, the City of Brotherly Love was the United States' biggest city and the center of its financial and artistic life well into the 19th century.

Originally home to the Lenapes and several other Native American nations, Pennsylvania was first colonized by Sweden in the 1630s. Fifty years later, English Quaker William Penn founded Pennsylvania as a haven for religious refugees. The colony and its capital city, Philadelphia, grew rapidly, and played a major role in both the Revolutionary War and the founding of the United States. In the 1800s, Pennsylvania underwent a revolution in transportation and industry, as enterprising people took advantage of the state's great natural resources.

The First Pennsylvanians

Hundreds of millions of years ago, great natural forces shaped the land that became the state of Pennsylvania. The landscape these forces created and the natural treasures they left behind have, in turn, shaped the lives of Pennsylvanians throughout the region's history.

Pressure from inside the earth, the movement of glaciers, and the action of wind and water built up the seven mountain ranges that stretch diagonally across the state, from the Poconos in the east to the Alleghenies in the west.

Between these mountains lie deep valleys. Together, these mountains and valleys are known as the Ridge-and-Valley Region. Many streams and waterways flow across the landscape, including three major river systems—the Delaware, the Ohio, and the Susquehanna. These rivers connect Pennsylvania with the Atlantic Ocean, the Great Lakes, and the Mississippi River, giving the state access to much of North America and to the sea. In addition, an eighty-mile-wide gap, the largest in the Appalachian mountain chain, exists in Pennsylvania, making overland travel easier and less time consuming.

At the western and eastern ends of the state are low-lying strips of land that harbor the state's most fertile soil. They have attracted farmers since colonial days.

Several times in its ancient history, Pennsylvania was flooded by a huge inland sea. The pressure of the sea turned the decaying remains of animals and plants into enormous deposits of coal and oil—minerals that would one day play an important role in the state's development.

People have lived in Pennsylvania for at least 12,000 years. The first Pennsylvanians were descendants of Asian peoples who came to North America across a bridge of land, long vanished, that once connected the two continents. Little is known about these ancient Pennsylvanians; all that remains of their settlements are fragments of stone tools and pottery. They were probably nomadic hunters, moving from place to place in search of game.

Eventually, Pennsylvania's Native Americans discovered how to grow crops—especially corn—and they began to settle in permanent homes along the region's streams and rivers.

By the time the first European explorers reached the region in the 17th century, about 20,000 Native Americans (or Indians, as the explorers mistakenly called them) lived in Pennsylvania and several distinct Native American cultures had developed in the region.

The land along the Delaware and Brandywine rivers was home to the Leni Lenapes. Their name means "the original people" in the Algonquian language, which was spoken by many Native American groups in northeastern North America. The first whites in Pennsylvania called them Delawares.

The Lenapes both hunted and farmed. Lenape men roamed the woods in search of deer and bears, while the women planted and harvested crops of corn, pumpkins, and beans. The Lenapes were a peaceful people, but they prized their independence. An early explorer reported that "[they] are a free people, subject to no one, but do what they please."

To the west, the Susquehannocks lived along the Susquehanna River. They spoke a branch of the Iroquoian language and were related to the Iroquois Confederacy, a powerful league of Native American nations in what is now New York. (Some other Iroquoian-speaking groups, like the Hurons, also lived in Pennsylvania.)

The Susquehannocks' way of life was much like the Lenapes', but instead of living in small huts like their eastern neighbors, the Susquehannocks built large, bark-roofed "longhouses," often with several rooms inside.

Several other Native American

This 18th-century woodcut of a *manitou* (spirit), is taken from a carving found over the entrance to a Lenape home. The Lenapes believed that everything in nature had its own manitou, which was either good or bad. This manitou may be the Great Horned Serpent, a figure of evil in the Lenape religion. The words "Manetto Indianorum" mean "Indian manitou" in Latin.

MANETTO INDIANORUM,

This figure of a Susquehannock Indian appears on a 1612 map drawn by English explorer Captain John Smith. The Susquehannocks were related both in language and lifestyle to the Iroquois Confederacy of present-day New York.

nations lived in western and southern Pennsylvania, including the Shawnee, Monongahela, and Erie tribes.

Even before white people came to Pennsylvania in large numbers, the region's Native Americans suffered the effects of white settlement.

In the mid-1600s, Dutch traders in New Netherland (now New York) began supplying the Iroquois with guns. Armed with these new and terrifying weapons, Iroquois war parties swept down into Pennsylvania. The Iroquois forced the peaceful Lenapes to hand over large sums of wampum (money made from clamshells) and to submit to Iroquois rule.

The Iroquois succeeded in conquering most of Pennsylvania's other Native American nations in a series of skirmishes known as the Beaver Wars. The Huron and Erie people were almost completely wiped out in wars with the Iroquois. The Susquehannocks held off the Iroquois for many years, but eventually they too were defeated. The surviving Susquehannocks were driven from their traditional homelands.

But a silent enemy even more deadly than Iroquois muskets devastated Pennsylvania's Indians in the 16th century: European diseases such as smallpox and measles. Because the Native Americans had no resistance to these unfamiliar illnesses, entire villages, even entire tribes, grew sick and died. Historians believe this was the fate of the Monongahelas, who suddenly disappeared around 1650.

It is unclear how many of Pennsylvania's Native Americans died in the wars with the Iroquois or from epidemics of disease. It is known, however, that in 1790, when the United States conducted its first national census, only about 1,000 Native Americans remained in Pennsylvania—just one-twentieth of the population that had existed 200 years before.

Early Exploration and Settlement

No one knows the identity of the first Europeans to set foot on Pennsylvania's shores. Fishermen in search of fresh water may have entered the mouth of the Delaware River in the 1500s. It is also possible that Giovanni da Verrazano, an Italian explorer sailing for France, saw the Delaware while charting the Atlantic Coast in 1524.

In the early 1600s, the Netherlands, France, and England began setting up colonies on the Atlantic Coast. Explorers from each of these countries entered Pennsylvania at one time or another, but none left much of a mark.

In 1608, Captain John Smith traveled north from Virginia in search of food for the English colony at Jamestown. Smith rowed up the Susquehanna River in a small boat, but it isn't clear if he got as far as Pennsylvania.

Another English explorer, Captain Samuel Argall, explored Delaware Bay two years later. Argall named the bay for Lord De La Warr, Virginia's governor. Henry Hudson, an English explorer sailing for the Dutch, sighted the Delaware River in 1609.

The first European known to have set foot in Pennsylvania was Dutch sea captain Cornelius Mey, who landed on the lower shores of the Delaware River in 1614.

The following year, Frenchman Etienne Brulé, traveling along the Susquehanna River, became the first explorer to see the hills and valleys of inland Pennsylvania. At about the same time, Dutch explorer Cornelius Hendrickson reached and named the Schuylkill River.

These early explorers found the region full of animals whose furs brought high prices in the markets of Europe. It wasn't long before European traders began to arrive in Pennsylvania, trading tools, guns, and other goods with the Native Americans in return for furs.

The first permanent settlement in Pennsylvania was founded by Sweden. In 1637, two ships carrying colonists and supplies dropped anchor in the Delaware River near present-day Wilmington, Delaware. It was not, however, an all-Swedish expedition: The colonists' leader, Peter Minuit, was Dutch (Minuit had already helped establish New Netherland), and many of the settlers were from Finland, which was then ruled by Sweden.

The settlers built a fort for protection, which they named Fort Christina (after Queen Christina of Sweden), and log cabins to live in. Log cabins were a common type of dwelling in the northern parts of Sweden and Finland, but this was the first time they appeared in North America. They would become the standard form of housing on the western frontier for more than two centuries.

The tiny Swedish settlement barely survived its first few years. The settlers soon ran short of food and probably would have starved without gifts of corn from the neighboring Lenapes. Finally, in 1640, supplies and more colonists arrived from Sweden.

The colony got a new governor—Johann Prinz, a soldier—in 1643. (Prinz, who weighed about 400 pounds, was given the name "Big Tub of Guts" by the Lenapes.) Prinz moved the colony up the Delaware to Tinicum Island (now part of the mainland) near present-day Philadelphia.

The Dutch in New Netherland looked on their Swedish-Finnish neighbors to the south as intruders on their territory and rivals for the profitable fur trade. Tension between the Dutch and the Swedes rose after the Swedes seized a Dutch trading post on the Delaware in 1654.

The following year, Peter Stuyvesant, governor of New Netherland, led a military expedition against the Swedes. On September 16, 1655, Stuyvesant forced them to raise the Dutch flag over Swedish settlements on the Delaware.

Dutch control of the region lasted less than a decade. In 1664, England captured New Netherland, and the land that would become Pennsylvania came under English rule.

New Sweden's most enduring legacy was the log cabin (above). Simple and sturdy, it required few tools and no nails to build. The log cabin was later adopted by German and Scottish-Irish settlers in Pennsylvania and eventually became a common frontier home in North America.

Shown here (left), a Swedish colonist trades with two Lenapes while others tend crops and fish in the Delaware River. This is a modern view of New Sweden, taken from a tapestry woven in the 1950s to celebrate Sweden's successful but short-lived American colony.

William Penn's "Holy Experiment"

In the mid-1600s, a new Protestant religious group appeared in England. Its members called themselves friends, and the group became known as the Society of Friends. Most people came to call the friends Quakers, supposedly because they "quaked (trembled) in the fear of the Lord."

The Quakers believed the "inner light" of God dwelled inside everyone. They did not worship in churches, they had no formal ministers, and they rejected many of the teachings of traditional Christianity, including baptism. The Quakers also opposed slavery and believed that war and violence were always wrong.

These beliefs were radical for the time. They soon brought the Quakers into conflict not only with the Church of England, which was backed by the power of the English government, but also with other Protestant groups, such as the Puritans. In England and in England's American colonies, Quakers were beaten, whipped, imprisoned, and sometimes killed.

Still, the power of the Quakers' ideas and the strength of their faith attracted thousands of converts. Among them was William Penn, a member of a wealthy English family,

The simplicity of the Quaker faith was expressed in their meeting houses, which were generally one-room wooden structures. In the meeting, each "friend," as the Quakers were called, spoke "as the Spirit moved" him or her, without a priest or minister to guide the service.

who became a Quaker in 1667 at the age of twenty-three.

Penn's father, Sir William Penn, had loaned a large sum of money to England's King Charles II, but he died before the king could pay him back. The money was now due to the younger William Penn, but instead he told the king that he would rather have a piece of land in North America.

Penn had long dreamed of a "holy experiment"—a colony that would allow Quakers and other persecuted religious groups to practice their religions without fear of attack. Now he had the chance to establish such a colony.

King Charles agreed. In 1681 he gave Penn control of about 50,000 square miles of land stretching westward from the Delaware River. Penn wanted to name the land New Wales or Sylvania ("the woods" in Latin), but the king insisted it be called Pennsylvania ("Penn's woods") to honor William Penn's father. Penn's

As a young man in London, William Penn was imprisoned twice for his Quaker beliefs: once for attending a Quaker meeting and a second time for preaching in the streets. He is shown here (top) later in life, after his "holy experiment" had become a thriving colony.

William Penn circulated pamphlets like this one (right) throughout Britain and Europe to encourage settlement in his colony. "Come to my province Pennsylvania, where you will find land you can own yourself, peace, freedom for worship in your own way, and a chance to take part in governing yourself," Penn wrote in one of them.

SOME
ACCOUNT
OF THE
PROVINCE
OF
PENNSILVANIA
IN
AMERICA;
Lately Granted under the Great Seal
OF
ENGLAND
TO
William Penn, &c.

Together with Priviledges and Powers necessary to the well-governing thereof.

Made publick for the Information of such as are or may be disposed to Transport themselves or Servants into those Parts.

LONDON: Printed, and Sold by Benjamin Clark Bookseller in George-Yard Lombard-street, 1681.

grant also included the present-day state of Delaware, but this area became a separate colony in 1703.

In September 1682, Penn arrived in Pennsylvania aboard the ship *Welcome* with 100 colonists, most of them Quakers. He was greeted by his cousin William Markham, who had gone on ahead to begin organizing the colony, and by the 400 or so Dutch, Swedish, and Finnish colonists who remained along the Delaware.

Penn chose a site near the point where the Schuylkill and Delaware rivers meet for the colony's major settlement. He named the site Philadelphia, which means City of Brotherly Love in classical Greek. The name reflected Penn's belief in tolerance for people of different religious faiths.

In December, Penn held a general assembly in the nearby settlement of Chester to organize a government for Pennsylvania.

According to the "First Frame" of government, which Penn had drafted while still living in England, laws would be made by an elected council and assembly. All male colonists who believed in God and owned at least a small amount of property could vote, and trial by jury and other rights were guaranteed.

By today's standards, some parts of the First Frame don't seem very democratic. As leader of the colony, for example, Penn (or a governor appointed by him) could veto—overturn—laws passed by the assembly and council. At a time when few people

anywhere in the world had any say in how they were governed, however, Pennsylvania's government was remarkably just. (Penn gave away part of his power as proprietor when the laws were revised in 1684 and more when they were revised again in 1701.)

Penn treated the local Native Americans with kindness and respect. Instead of just taking land that belonged to them, Penn—whom the Indians called *Onas*, the Algonquian word for pen—negotiated treaties with Native American groups and paid them for their land.

In 1701, representatives from several Native American groups visited Philadelphia and signed a treaty of friendship with Penn. The French philosopher Voltaire called the agreement "the only treaty never sworn to"—Quakers refused to swear oaths—"and never broken."

William Penn spent a total of only three years in Pennsylvania—from 1682 to 1684 and again from 1699 to 1701. By the time he died in 1718, however, Penn had seen his colony become a symbol of hope to the world.

The Growth of the Quaker Colony

In the decades after the *Welcome* dropped anchor in the Delaware River, thousands of poor and persecuted people from all over Europe came to Pennsylvania, attracted by the promise of religious tolerance and the chance to make a better life for themselves. The colony had a population of about 500 in 1682; just two decades later it had grown to more than 20,000 people.

In Pennsylvania's first years, most of the settlers were Quakers and other religious "dissenters" from England and Wales, along with some Huguenots (French Protestants). The Quakers included many people who had been craftsworkers or merchants in their homeland, and they tended to settle in and around Philadelphia.

Settlers from Germany formed the next big group of immigrants to arrive in Pennsylvania. So many settled in the colony that about half of Pennsylvania's population was German-speaking by the middle of the 18th

This birth certificate is written in the beautiful *fraktur* script developed by the Pennsylvania Dutch, who began to arrive in the colony in the late 1600s. (*Fraktur* comes from a German word meaning "broken.")

century. Some German colonists were members of religious groups like the Amish and Mennonites. These "Plain People," as they came to be called, lived simple and pious lives. Most German immigrants, however, were Lutherans or members of Reformed (Calvinist Protestant) churches.

The Germans settled mostly in eastern Pennsylvania, especially in York and Lancaster counties. These Pennsylvania Dutch—the name comes from the word *Deutsch*, which means German—became famous for their cooking, hospitality, efficient farms, and unique crafts.

A third group of immigrants were the Scottish-Irish—Protestants (mostly Presbyterian) who had originally settled in northern Ireland. These hardy people preferred to live on the frontier, and throughout the 18th century they pushed steadily into western Pennsylvania—the part of the colony lying west of the Susquehanna River.

By the middle of the 18th century, Philadelphia was not only the largest city in Britain's North American colonies, but the second-largest English-speaking city (after London) in the world. William Penn had planned the city as a "green country town," and it was laid out carefully, with wide

Ships crowd the Delaware River in this 1751 view of Philadelphia, which by this time was the commercial and cultural capital of Britain's American colonies, and the largest city in North America.

The naturalist John Bartram's son, William, followed in his father's botanical footsteps and was thought by many to be a more gifted artist. He spent much of his life tending and sketching plants (left) in his father's extensive garden near Philadelphia.

This lithograph (below) depicts the famous 1762 experiment in which Benjamin Franklin proved that lightning was electricity. Besides his pioneering studies of electricity, Franklin was responsible for inventions like the Franklin stove, an unusual musical instrument called the glass harmonica, and bifocal glasses.

streets and plenty of parks. One 18th-century visitor described the town as "grandeur and perfection. . . . Its fine appearance, good regulations, agreeable situation, natural advantages, trade, riches, and power are by no means inferior to any, even the most ancient towns of Europe."

The city was also the cultural center of the colonies. Philadelphia in the 18th century was home to such remarkable residents as naturalist John Bartram, who planted America's first botanical garden just outside the city in 1728, and scientist Benjamin Rush, who founded the Pennsylvania Hospital, the first hospital in the colonies, in 1751.

The most remarkable Philadelphian of all was Benjamin Franklin, a man who had arrived in the city from Boston as a penniless teenager in 1723. Finding work as a printer, Franklin began publishing *The Pennsylvania Gazette* newspaper in 1729. A few years later he wrote and published the first edition of *Poor Richard's Almanac*, a witty, widely read publication that made Franklin famous. His work *Proposals Relating to the Education of Youth in Pennsylvania*, published in 1749, led to the founding of the Academy of Philadelphia, later known as the University of Pennsylvania.

In addition to Franklin's interest in publishing, he devoted much of his life to politics and to the study of natural science. He served on the committee for the drafting of the Declaration of Independence and in 1776 was sent to France as one of three representatives of the thirteen colonies. As a scientist, he conducted many experiments with static electricity and atmospheric pressure, and was the inventor of the highly-efficient Franklin stove.

While Philadelphia prospered, trouble brewed on Pennsylvania's western frontier. In the early 1750s, France, which at this time ruled Canada and claimed much of the North American interior, began building a string of forts along the southern shore of Lake Erie.

The French presence was a threat to British control of the region, but the Pennsylvania Assembly, controlled by antiwar Quakers, would not allow military action. Finally, in 1753, the colony of Virginia sent a young officer, Lieutenant Colonel George Washington, through the Pennsylvania wilderness with a letter demanding France's withdrawal. The commander at the chief French post, Fort Le Boeuf, refused the demand.

The following year, the French captured a small British outpost at the point where the Ohio, Allegheny, and Monongahela rivers meet. They named this strategic spot Fort Duquesne (pronounced "du-caine").

In the spring of 1754, Washington clashed with French forces near Fort Duquesne. This wilderness skirmishing touched off the conflict known in America as the French and Indian War—a struggle between Britain and France for control of North America.

In 1755, a British attempt to recapture Fort Duquesne ended in disaster when French troops and their Indian allies ambushed a British force. Three years later, however, defeats elsewhere led the French to abandon Fort Duquesne. The British rebuilt the post and named it Fort Pitt after British prime minister William Pitt.

A defiant Pontiac faces British and Pennsylvania officials in this engraving. In 1766, two years after his defeat at Bushy Run, Pontiac signed a peace treaty with the British. He mysteriously died three years later, probably at the hands of a Native American hired by the British.

The war ended with France's defeat in 1763, but conflict continued in western Pennsylvania, this time between Native Americans and colonists.

The good relations established by William Penn between whites and Native Americans lasted only a few decades after his death. The leaders that followed Penn, including his sons, were not as respectful of Native American rights. In the famous "walking purchase" of 1737, for example, the Lenapes agreed to sell the colony a parcel of land extending west "as far as a man can walk in a day and a half." The colonists took unfair advantage of this agreement by using relays of runners to mark out the territory, instead of one man walking at a normal pace.

The hunger for land soon drove the colony's surviving Native Americans into ever-smaller territories, and many fought back by raiding settlements on the frontier. In the aftermath of the French and Indian War, these hit-and-run attacks gave way to an all-out attempt to drive the British from western Pennsylvania.

Pontiac, a chief of the Huron nation, led several tribes against the British forts and settlements south of Lake Erie. Pontiac almost succeeded in capturing Fort Pitt, but soldiers led by Henry Bouquet, a Swiss soldier serving with the British, broke through and defeated Pontiac's warriors in the Battle of Bushy Run in August 1763.

Birthplace of the United States

The French and Indian War was an expensive victory for Britain. To pay off the debts brought on by the war and to raise money for the defense of its North American empire, the British government began to tax the thirteen colonies.

These taxes and trade regulations met with spirited protests in the colonies. Many Patriots, as colonists who were against the taxes came to be known, felt that Britain had no right to tax the colonies because the colonies had no representatives in the British Parliament.

Many Pennsylvanians protested against such British measures as the Stamp Act of 1766 and the Townshend Acts of 1767. Lawyer John Dickinson won many supporters for the Patriot cause with his "Letters from a Pennsylvania Farmer," a series of writings that appeared in newspapers throughout the colonies in 1767 and 1768.

As a result of Patriot protests, Parliament ended some of the taxes. In the early 1770s, however, relations again grew tense when Parliament introduced a tax on imported tea. In Boston, Patriots tossed crates of tea into the harbor in the famous Boston Tea Party. There was no tea party in Pennsylvania: Philadelphia Patriots simply invited the captain of the British tea ship *Polly* to a protest meeting. The strength of the Patriots' convictions convinced the captain not to even try to bring his cargo into port.

Not all Pennsylvanians took part in the protests. The colony's governor, John Penn (William Penn's grandson), was firmly pro-British. So were many Philadelphia merchants, who didn't want to see trade with Britain disrupted. Despite the efforts of Governor Penn and his supporters, however, the Patriots gained ground in the assembly.

Pennsylvania was the site of the First Continental Congress, an assembly of leading Patriots from all the colonies. The congress, which met in Philadelphia's Carpenter's Hall from September 5 to October 6, 1774, voted to continue the protests against Parliament and to meet again the following spring.

By that time, however, protest had given way to fighting after British troops and armed Patriots clashed at the towns of Lexington and Concord, Massachusetts. Many Patriots decided that complete independence from Britain was the only course of action left to take.

The Second Continental Congress, held in Philadelphia's State House, opened in May 1776. One of its leaders was Benjamin Franklin, just returned to Pennsylvania after years in Britain as the colony's representative.

Franklin was a member of the committee that drafted the Declaration of Independence—the document that officially cut the ties between Britain and its rebellious colonies. Approved on July 4, the declaration was read aloud to cheering crowds in front of the State House on July 8.

The Revolutionary War came to Pennsylvania in August 1777, when British troops landed along the shores of Chesapeake Bay. The main Patriot fighting force, the Continental Army—led by George Washington, whose first taste of combat had been on the Pennsylvania frontier in 1754—tried to stop the British advance at Brandywine Creek. Washington was forced to retreat, however, and the British won another victory at Paoli a week later.

On September 25, 1777, British troops, together with Hessian mercenaries (German soldiers paid by a foreign government to fight), marched into Philadelphia. Washington attacked suburban Germantown in an attempt to force the British out of the city, but the assault failed when heavy fog blanketed the battlefield.

While the British occupied Philadelphia and Congress fled to York, the Continental Army went into winter quarters at Valley Forge, about twenty miles from Philadelphia. Here, the soldiers endured a grim winter that was perhaps the low point of the

This 1816 painting by John Trumbull shows Thomas Jefferson presenting the Declaration of Independence to the Second Continental Congress on July 4, 1776. The document was voted on and approved that day, but most of the delegates didn't sign the declaration until August 2. Benjamin Franklin is shown standing to Jefferson's right.

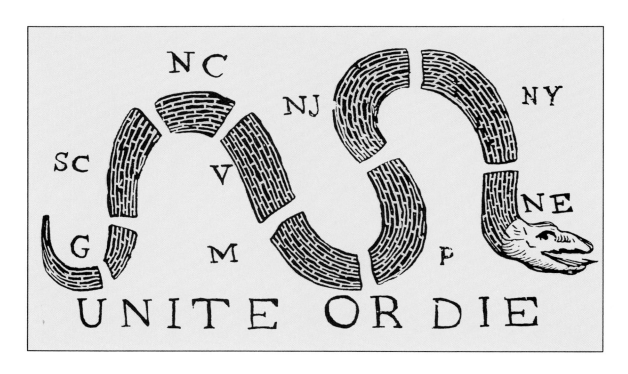

war. Nearly 3,000 men died of starvation, disease, and exposure.

Washington's leadership held the army together, however. When the soldiers marched out of Valley Forge in June 1778, they were finally a skilled, disciplined fighting force, thanks to training by Friedrich von Steuben, a German officer who had come to help the Patriot cause.

On June 19, the British left Philadelphia. In central Pennsylvania, however, a particularly brutal and bitter conflict broke out.

Here, pro-British settlers and their Iroquois allies attacked settlements along the upper Susquehanna River. Seeking protection, terrified settlers and their families crowded into a small outpost called Forty Fort in the Wyoming Valley near present-day Wilkes-Barre. On July 5 the Iroquois attacked, and about 200 settlers—including many women and children—

were killed in what became known as the Wyoming Massacre.

In 1783, a peace treaty ended the conflict and guaranteed American independence. A new nation, the United States, had been born. In a sense, the new country's birthplace was Pennsylvania. It was in Philadelphia that independence had been declared, and Pennsylvanians had played important roles in all parts of the struggle against Britain.

At least 35,000 Pennsylvanians and perhaps many more fought with the Continental Army or in militia (local) units. Two Philadelphia businessmen, Haym Solomon and Robert Morris, were the leading financiers of the war, and the colony gave $7.5 million to the Patriot cause. Finally, the grain, gunpowder, lead, and iron provided by Pennsylvania went a long way toward feeding and arming the Continental Army.

Four years after the war's end, Philadelphia's State House—now known as Independence Hall—was again the site of a historic meeting. This time, delegates from all but one of the newly independent states gathered to form an effective national government. The document that came out of this convention, the United States Constitution, still governs the nation more than two centuries later. Pennsylvania's assembly ratified (approved) the Constitution in December 1787—the second state to do so.

First published by Benjamin Franklin in 1754 with the slogan "Join or die," this cartoon (opposite, top) again became popular around the time of the American Revolution. With the saying changed to "Unite or die," it urged the thirteen colonies to come together and defeat the British in the war for American independence.

Cold, weary, hungry, and sick, Continental soldiers huddle around a fire at Valley Forge in this engraving (left). Nearly 3,000 soldiers died at the camp during the winter of 1777–78, most of them from disease. "God grant we may never be brought to such a wretched condition again!" wrote one of Washington's generals when the ordeal ended.

Postwar Problems and Progress

Philadelphia became the new national capital in 1776, when the colonies declared their independence from England, and remained so until 1800, when the seat of government was moved to the District of Columbia.

One unpleasant fact of life in the new capital was disease. Philadelphia had long suffered epidemics of yellow fever in the summer heat, and anyone who could afford to built a summer house in the cooler suburbs. The yellow fever season of 1792 was especially devastating; the disease killed nearly 5,000 Philadelphians, almost 10 percent of the city's total population.

While President Washington and Congress moved into their new quarters in Philadelphia, the state's borders were changed to what they are today. The boundary between Pennsylvania and Maryland had been surveyed by 1763 (the boundary became famous as the "Mason-Dixon Line," named after its chief surveyors), but several other states, including Massachusetts, New York, and Connecticut,

When the nation's capital moved to Philadelphia, this "presidential mansion" was built at Ninth and Market streets. The building later became part of the University of Pennsylvania, but was destroyed in 1829.

claimed a wedge-shaped strip of land along Lake Erie.

As the 18th century came to a close, Pennsylvania experienced a political struggle between wealthy landowners and frontier settlers. During the Revolutionary War, the new state of Pennsylvania had adopted a somewhat radical state constitution. Among other things, the 1776 constitution gave the state a unicameral (one house) legislature and replaced a single governor with an elected Executive Council.

The constitution had the support of most of Pennsylvania's small farmers and frontier settlers, who believed the document took power from the hands of the small group of wealthy merchants and landowners who had ruled

Artist and architect Benjamin Latrobe painted this view of a rural Pennsylvania farm in 1801. The painting shows the rugged terrain that made travel into and out of western Pennsylvania so difficult and time-consuming.

Pennsylvania for decades. Pennsylvania's unusual system of government proved impractical, however. In 1790, a new and more conservative constitution was adopted, but not without opposition from the many Pennsylvanians who believed it would be controlled by the state's "landed and mercantile (business)" interests.

The federal government took control of the 200,000-acre Erie Triangle, as it was called, and in 1792 the government sold the land to the state of Pennsylvania. The purchase of the

Western Pennsylvania farmers used simple stills, like the one shown here, to turn bulky rye and corn into easily transportable whiskey. The 1791 law taxed whiskey at a rate of 54 cents per gallon, and many distillers claimed they had to pay more in taxes for their whiskey than they could get by selling it.

Erie Triangle had a great impact on the state's development because it gave Pennsylvania access to the Great Lakes, the hub of North America's inland waterways.

Settlement in western Pennsylvania increased after the Revolutionary War, especially as veterans and their families moved onto "donation lands" given to them as payment for their service. Still, the new settlements west of the Susquehanna River were isolated from the rest of the state, because there were no roads through the mountain ranges that crisscross the region. It wasn't until 1783, for example, that the first wagon train made it from the east to the settlement at the site of old Fort Pitt. The settlement, now known as Pittsburgh, was, in the words of a visitor, no more than "sixty wooden houses and cabins in which live something more than one hundred families."

This transportation problem led to one of the first important challenges to the federal government's authority—the Whiskey Rebellion. It was much easier for farmers in western Pennsylvania to distill their crops of corn and rye into whiskey than to transport the grain itself across the mountains to market. In 1791, however, the federal government, which was desperately short of money, announced a steep tax on whiskey.

The frontiersmen refused to pay the tax, chased away the federal agents sent to collect it, and threatened to attack Pittsburgh. In 1794, President Washington ordered that a force of 13,000 men be raised and then he personally led this army into the mountains of western Pennsylvania.

This show of force convinced the farmers to back down, as did the arrest of twenty leading "anti-tax rebels." The rebellion ended with only one death, and the imprisoned leaders were soon released.

Pennsylvanians faced another danger during the War of 1812 when the United States went to war with its former colonial ruler, Britain. American control of the Great Lakes was vital to the nation's defense, but the United States had no navy on the lakes. Pennsylvania took on the task of building one. Carpenters, crafts-workers, sailors, and a handful of naval officers made the difficult journey across the state to the small town of Erie.

In an amazing feat of construction, a fleet of small warships was built and launched in just a few weeks. On September 10, 1813, the fleet sailed into battle against the British. The U.S. commander, Oliver Hazard Perry, skillfully maneuvered his ships and the Americans were victorious. The Battle of Lake Erie was a bright spot in the War of 1812—a war that saw many American defeats.

Their sails full of holes left by cannonballs, British and American warships shoot each other at close range during the Battle of Lake Erie on September 10, 1813. After the battle, Captain Oliver Hazard Perry announced his victory with the famous message, "We have met the enemy and they are ours."

Transportation and Industry

Once the leading American city in all respects, Philadelphia began to lose its national importance in the first decades of the 19th century. By 1810, New York had passed Philadelphia to become the nation's largest city. And Philadelphia was no longer Pennsylvania's capital: The state government moved to York in 1799 and then to Harrisburg in 1812, where it remains today.

While Philadelphia declined in importance in the first half of the 19th century, Pennsylvania as a state experienced great growth and change during this era. Revolutions in transportation and industry took hold in the United States, and Pennsylvania, with its excellent geographical position and abundant natural resources, played an important role in both.

Businesspeople and politicians had long known that Pennsylvania's transportation network, especially roads, needed improvement if the state's economy was to prosper.

Pennsylvania's first major turnpike, or toll road, was the seventy-mile Philadelphia-Lancaster Turnpike, which opened in 1794. Paved with wood, stone, and gravel, it was the first hard-surface road in the United States. Over the next four decades, 3,000 miles of road were built throughout the state, and after 1804 stagecoaches and freight wagons traveled regularly between Philadelphia and Pittsburgh.

One product of Pennsylvania's ever increasing system of roads was the massive Conestoga wagon. Invented in Lancaster County, one wagon could transport between 2,000 and 3,000 pounds of produce from the region's farms to towns and cities along the turnpike.

The development of the steamboat gave a boost to transportation on Pennsylvania's excellent river system. As early as 1790, Philadelphia inventor John Fitch was operating a steam ferry service between Philadelphia and Burlington, New Jersey. In the early 1800s, another Pennsylvanian, Robert Fulton, came up with a more practical design for a steam-powered vessel.

Fulton's first successful steamboat, the *Clermont*, went into local service on the Hudson River, and in 1812 one of his steamboats chugged all the way from Pittsburgh to New Orleans down the Mississippi River.

The rise of the state's coal and iron industries helped spur Pennsylvania's transportation revolution. In the first decades of the century, miners began to mine eastern Pennsylvania's deposits of anthracite (hard coal) for use in heating and industry.

Pennsylvania had produced iron since the Quaker era. The colony's first iron forge was constructed in 1716, and as early as 1681 William Penn alluded to iron in a pamphlet promoting manufacturing possibilities in Pennsylvania. But it was the discovery of soft (bituminous) coal in the western part of the state that actually made Pennsylvania one of the world's leading iron producers. This is because bituminous coal can be converted into coke, a vital ingredient in the iron and steel-making process. Thanks to nearby deposits of coal and iron ore, Pittsburgh quickly became the center of the state's iron industry.

The state's transportation network expanded to include many canals to transport freight (especially coal) and passengers. By the mid-1800s the Schuylkill Canal alone, which linked the eastern Pennsylvania anthracite coal fields to New York and Philadelphia, carried 1.5 million tons of coal each year.

So many canals were built that people began to talk of "canal fever," and in 1825 the state government stepped in to coordinate private canal-building activities. Work on a canal link between Philadelphia and Pittsburgh began a year later.

This painting depicts a typical scene on a Pennsylvania canal around 1830. Canal boats were wide, flat-bottomed vessels, usually pulled by a team of mules on the towpath that ran alongside the canal. When weather permitted, passengers rode on deck instead of staying inside the canal boat's cabin, which was often cramped and uncomfortable.

The sheet music to an anti-immigrant Nativist song proclaims "Citizen Know-Nothing" as "Uncle Sam's Youngest Son." The American Party, as the Know-Nothings were officially called, enjoyed great strength in Philadelphia, and in the congressional elections of 1854 the party's candidates won 40 percent of the vote in Pennsylvania.

The centerpiece of the Pennsylvania Main Line Canal system was the Allegheny Portage Railroad, a system of inclined planes that carried canal boats across the mountainous gap between the eastern and western ends of the canal. In 1834, when the system was finished, travel time for the 300 miles between the two cities was cut from as long as a month to about five days.

Before long, however, railroads began to replace canals as the most important part of Pennsylvania's transportation system. In 1829, the first commercial railroad in the United States linked Carbondale and Honesdale. Within ten years, Pennsylvania had more than a quarter of all the railroad track in the country.

Farm and forest products remained vital to Pennsylvania's economy, but more and more Pennsylvanians were now working in mines, mills, and factories. Work in these new industries usually meant long hours, low pay, and often dangerous conditions. With few laws to protect them and business owners who were mostly deaf to their complaints, workers began to form unions to win better treatment.

As early as 1827, workers in Philadelphia organized the Mechanics' Union of Trade Associations, one of the first important labor groups in the United States. Most of the efforts of this and other groups, however, were unsuccessful, because strikes and other tactics were considered "illegal combinations" under Pennsylvania law.

Growing numbers of these new industrial workers were immigrants from overseas, especially Ireland. Besides the difficulties and dangers of the workplace, these immigrants faced prejudice from some native-born Pennsylvanians. These "Nativists" feared "contamination" of what they considered traditional American culture by immigrants and Roman Catholics.

Some of these Nativists joined political groups like the American Party, better known as the Know-Nothings, because members were ordered to reveal nothing if questioned about the group's activities. In May 1844, Nativists attacked immigrant neighborhoods and churches in Philadelphia. The rioting became so fierce that the governor had to call in the state militia to restore order.

Around the time of the Philadelphia riots, a Pittsburgh pharmacist named Samuel Kier made an important discovery. For years, people had noticed petroleum—oil—seeping from rocks in the area. This oil was sometimes bottled and sold as medicine. Kier, however, found that when distilled, oil would produce a clear, bright light in lamps when ignited. People realized that this new fuel could replace the expensive whale oil then used for lighting. Production of carbon fuel, or kerosene, was soon a profitable industry.

In 1859, Edwin Drake, a former railroad conductor, sunk a well seventy feet into the soil near the northwestern Pennsylvania town of Titusville. Black liquid spouted from the end of his drill—Drake had brought in the nation's first "gusher." An oil rush swept across western Pennsylvania, much like the gold rush that hit California a decade before. The boom died down by 1891, but Pennsylvania remained a leading oil-producing state for decades.

Oil gushes from a well that has been "shot"—rigged with explosives—in this photograph from the early days of Pennsylvania's oil boom. By 1890 the state was exporting more than 30 million barrels of oil each year.

MODERN PENNSYLVANIA

This painting by Carl Walberg shows a Pittsburgh steelworker pouring molten metal into a mold. By 1900 the state's steel mills employed 110,000 workers who produced more than half of all the steel made in the United States.

In July 1863, the three-day Battle of Gettysburg—the turning point of the Civil War—was fought in Pennsylvania. In the decades that followed, Pennsylvania's steel plants, coal mines, factories, and oil refineries made the state an industrial and economic giant, but only at the cost of great struggle between workers and business owners. In the 20th century, the state suffered through the Great Depression of the 1930s, made great contributions to the war effort in both world wars, and coped with a changing economy and population. With its new high-tech industries and wealth of natural and human resources, modern Pennsylvania remains, in many important ways, the Keystone State of American life.

Pennsylvania and the Civil War

By 1860, Pennsylvania had a population of nearly 3 million people. More than 400,000 of these Pennsylvanians, or about 15 percent of the population, were immigrants.

The year 1860 was a fateful one for Pennsylvania and for the entire nation. Abraham Lincoln, candidate of the new, antislavery Republican Party, was elected president. Tensions between the slaveowning states of the South and the free (nonslave) states of the North had been rising for years. With Lincoln's election, Southern states began to secede (leave) from the Union to form a new country called the Confederate States of America.

Pennsylvania was founded on the idea of freedom, and many of its citizens were against slavery. The Quakers opposed slavery and forbade slaveholding members from attending their meetings. German-speaking religious groups like the Mennonites also considered slavery evil. In 1780, Pennsylvania became one of the first states to outlaw slavery by declaring all African Americans born in the state free.

Because of its location bordering Maryland and Virginia (both of which were slave states), Pennsylvania was also a key link in the Underground Railroad, the network of antislavery activists who smuggled escaped slaves to freedom.

President-elect Lincoln passed through Pennsylvania on his way to Washington in March 1861. Stopping in Philadelphia, he gave a stirring speech at Independence Hall. "There shall be no bloodshed," said Lincoln about the secession of the Southern states, "unless it be forced on the government."

But there was to be much bloodshed. It began a month later when Confederate cannons shelled the union-held fort in the harbor at Charleston, South Carolina. When the news reached Pennsylvania, 350 volunteer soldiers—later famous as the "first defenders"—rushed to Washington to protect the capital. Over the course of four years of war, they were followed by about 380,000 Pennsylvania troops. Probably one in ten died in combat or of disease or wounds.

Pennsylvania's farms and industries also did much to aid the Union war effort. Historians estimate that three quarters of the cannons and rails used by Union forces came from the state's ironworks.

The turning point of the war took place in Pennsylvania. In June 1863, Confederate general Robert E. Lee led the Army of the Potomac, the chief Confederate fighting force, across the Potomac River into Pennsylvania in a bold gamble to win the war by invading the North.

Nothing stood between Lee's army and Washington, D.C., except Union general George Meade's Army of the

Potomac. The Philadelphia-born Meade found himself defending his home state.

On July 1, units of both armies clashed in the town of Gettysburg. Lee's Confederates captured the town, but Meade rushed reinforcements to the high ground around Gettysburg.

Fierce fighting swirled around the hills and fields near Gettysburg throughout the blazing hot day of July 2. Night fell with the Union defenders still holding their positions.

The climax of the battle came on July 3, when Lee sent 15,000 men, under the command of General George Pickett, in a massive charge against the Union lines. The Confederates swept forward and nearly broke through the Union ranks, but the charge finally broke up under withering Union artillery and rifle fire, and the survivors staggered back to their own positions.

Lee realized his gamble had failed. On July 4, he began withdrawing his battered army toward safety in Maryland. Some 50,000 men on both sides had been killed or wounded in the battle—the largest battle ever fought on American soil.

In the aftermath of that battle, seventeen acres of land at Gettysburg were set aside as a national cemetery for the Union troops who had died there. A Gettysburg citizen, David Wills, invited President Lincoln to deliver "a few appropriate remarks" at

General George Pickett (above) gave his name to the charge at Gettysburg, although as a division commander he remained behind and did not lead his troops into battle. "General, I have no division now," said a tearful Pickett to Lee as the few survivors of the charge returned to the Confederate lines.

This lithograph (left) shows Pickett's charge as seen from the Union lines on Cemetery Ridge. The Confederates lost 7,500 men in this brave but failed attempt to break through the Union defenders and win the Battle of Gettysburg. Of the Confederate officers who led the charge, there was not a single man above the rank of captain who was not wounded or killed.

the cemetery's dedication. Lincoln accepted, and on November 19 he arrived in Gettysburg for the ceremony.

The three-minute speech Lincoln gave received only polite applause from the crowd; the president himself called it "a flat failure." Still, Lincoln's brief but moving tribute to the men who had fallen and to the spirit of democracy stirred the nation. Lincoln's Gettysburg Address has passed into history as one of the greatest speeches of all time.

After Gettysburg, the North was never again seriously threatened by a Confederate invasion. A year after the battle, however, Southern soldiers again set foot in Pennsylvania when Confederate cavalry raided the town of Chambersburg. When the towns-

Lincoln's Gettysburg Address was so short that a photographer didn't even have time to photograph the president making his speech. He captured Lincoln, hatless and left of center, just as he stood up, but by the time the photographer was ready to shoot again, the speech was over.

people refused to pay a "ransom" of $100,000 in gold, the Confederates burned most of the town.

The war ended in April 1865 with Lee's surrender to Union commander Ulysses S. Grant. Pennsylvania and its people had done much to make the Union victory possible. In the words of one state historian: "The total contribution made by Pennsylvania to the North's victory is so considerable and so varied as to justify its reputation as the keystone state of the Civil War."

Coal, Steel, and Strikes

Pennsylvania's population doubled in the years between the end of the Civil War and the turn of the 20th century, from about 3 million to more than 6 million people. Much of this growth came from immigration—among the states, only New York had a higher percentage of foreign-born citizens in 1900.

Unlike the waves of German and Irish immigrants that had settled in Pennsylvania in the 18th and mid-19th centuries, these newcomers came mostly from eastern, southern, and central Europe—places like Russia, Hungary, Italy, Poland, and Yugoslavia.

The immigrants provided much of the labor for the mines, mills, and factories that made Pennsylvania an industrial leader. The industrial revolution that began in the years before the Civil War went into high gear when that conflict ended. It was a time when enterprising businesspeople made vast fortunes and created great industrial empires—and an era in which ordinary workers waged bitter and often violent struggles for better treatment in the workplace.

Pittsburgh was the centerpiece of the state's industrial heartland. By 1870, half of all the iron used in the country was produced in the city. The 1873 development of the Bessemer process, an improved method for making steel, heightened the city's reputation as the nation's steel capital.

The rise of Pittsburgh's steel industry was largely the work of Andrew Carnegie, whose life story reads like a classic "rags to riches" tale. Arriving with his poor family from Scotland in 1848, the thirteen-year-old immigrant found work in a cotton mill for $1.25 a week. By the time he was thirty, the hard-working, thrifty Carnegie controlled several factories and mills. It was Carnegie who introduced the

Together with Henry Clay Frick, Scottish-born Andrew Carnegie (below) created the greatest industrial corporation to emerge from Pittsburgh's steel mills. Today, Carnegie is remembered as much for his charitable works as for his brilliant business ability.

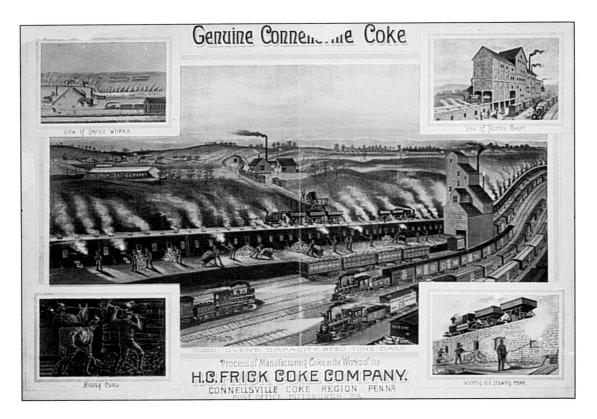

Genuine Connellsville Coke

View of Bravo Works.

View of Trotter Shaft.

Process of Manufacturing Coke at the Works of the
H.C.FRICK COKE COMPANY.
CONNELLSVILLE COKE REGION PENNA
POST OFFICE PITTSBURGH PA

Mining Coal

Watering and Drawing Coke

This lithograph shows the "beehive" ovens in which coal was baked into coke, a coal by-product that is mostly carbon. Coke is an essential ingredient in the recipe for steel, and Henry Clay Frick's control of Pittsburgh's coke supply made him a valued ally of Andrew Carnegie.

Bessemer process to America, and he built huge plants at Homestead and Braddock to manufacture steel using the new technology.

Carnegie needed a steady supply of coal and coke (coal residue used as fuel) for his blast furnaces, but almost all the coal and coke in the Pittsburgh area was controlled by Henry Clay Frick, a brilliant businessman of Penn-sylvania Dutch background. Carnegie convinced Frick to join him, and the resulting corporation, the Carnegie Steel Company, quickly conquered the market for steel.

While Carnegie and Frick established their empire, labor trouble broke out in the anthracite coal fields of eastern Pennsylvania. Here, boys as young as six or seven years old worked as "breaker boys," picking coal from slag (waste rock). If they survived, they began working in the mines at age twelve or thirteen, spending long hours underground in conditions that were unbelievably dangerous. Everyday, miners faced fires, mine collapses, crippling injuries, and lung diseases.

As a result of these brutal working conditions, miners rebelled by forming a secret society known as the Molly Maguires. Founded before the Civil War, the Molly Maguires turned to violence in the 1870s. A historian described their activities: "They attacked superintendents, murdered mine bosses, and put the fear of death . . . into judges and police."

In 1875, the Miners and Laborers Benevolent Association, an early miners' union, called a strike. How much the Molly Maguires had to do with the strike is still not known, but mine owners seized the chance to both break the strike and destroy the power of the Molly Maguires. Trainloads of strikebreakers (non-union workers) arrived in the coalfields, and private detectives were hired to secretly join the Molly Maguires.

After five months, the strike collapsed, and the striking miners—or at least those not permanently barred from the mines—were hired back with a large pay cut. The detectives gathered enough evidence about the Molly Maguires' activities to bring five of them to trial for the murder of a policeman. All were found guilty and hanged in May 1876.

The last decade of the 19th century saw more struggles between the growing labor movement and the state's industrial giants.

The first took place in 1892, when

One of the worst disasters in American history, the Johnstown Flood, struck Pennsylvania on May 31, 1889. The Southfork Dam, which held back the waters of the Conemaugh and Stony Creek rivers, burst, sending 20 million tons of water crashing through the western Pennsylvania community of Johnstown, fourteen miles to the west. At least 2,200 people died in the tragedy and another 1,000 were listed as missing.

workers at Carnegie Steel's Homestead plant went on strike to protest, among other things, their twelve-hour a day, seven-day work week. Carnegie was in Europe at the time, leaving Henry Clay Frick to handle the strike.

Frick refused to negotiate with the strikers or even to recognize their

union. Like the mine owners during the 1875 anthracite strike, he brought in non-union workers to run the blast furnaces and private detectives to protect the plant and the strikebreakers. The strike turned violent on July 6, when strikers and detectives traded gunfire in a day-long Battle of Homestead that left ten people dead and hundreds injured.

Three days later, Governor Robert Pattison sent 8,000 troops into Homestead to keep the peace. Later that month, Frick survived an assassination attempt but still did not give in to the strikers. In November the strike ended when the union gave in to Frick's terms.

If conditions in the steel plants of Pittsburgh were bad, life in the anthracite fields was worse. Between 1870 and 1900, for example, nearly 10,000 miners lost their lives while working in the mines.

Improving the lives of the anthracite miners was the goal of John Mitchell, founder of the United Mine Workers (UMW) Union. By 1897, Mitchell succeeded in bringing most of the miners into the UMW.

Five years later, 150,000 UMW members walked off the job. They remained on strike for five months. Although the strike was peaceful, neither the mine owners nor the union could reach an agreement. As winter approached, the strike became an issue of national concern, because much of the coal needed to heat the nation's homes came from the anthracite fields.

Finally, President Theodore Roosevelt stepped in and called on both sides to negotiate a settlement, which they did. The 1902 anthracite strike marked the first use of presidential power to solve a labor dispute. It was a major victory for organized labor, not just in Pennsylvania, but for the entire nation.

At the end of the Battle of Homestead (opposite) on July 6, 1892, the 300 Pinkerton detectives hired by Frick surrendered to the strikers and were marched through the town of Homestead. The Pinkertons were later replaced by 8,000 troops sent by Pennsylvania governor Robert Pattison.

On July 23, 1892, Henry Frick was seriously wounded when a young anarchist, Alexander Berkman (right), shot him twice and stabbed him repeatedly with a file in his office. Berkman spent fourteen years in jail for the attack.

Pennsylvania in the 20th Century

Coal, oil, iron, and steel continued to drive Pennsylvania's economy in the 20th century.

In 1901, Andrew Carnegie capped his career by overseeing the establishment of the U.S. Steel Corporation. This industrial giant, the biggest corporation in the world at the time, controlled not only 149 steel mills, but also mines, railroads, and fleets of ships—all the elements needed to produce, transport, and market steel.

The business deal that created U.S. Steel was arranged by Carnegie's trusted associate, Charles M. Schwab. Like Carnegie, Schwab was a self-made man who had begun his career as an ordinary laborer. Two years after forming U.S. Steel, however, Schwab founded his own steel company, Bethlehem Steel, which quickly became U.S. Steel's chief competitor.

Andrew Carnegie spent the rest of his life giving away much of the vast wealth he had gained as Pennsylvania's greatest industrialist. "He who dies rich, dies disgraced," said Carnegie, and by the time he died in 1919, Carnegie had donated $350 million to various charities. Much of the money went to build 2,500 libraries around the country.

In the first decades of the new century, however, many Pennsylvanians felt that industrialists like Carnegie and Schwab had too much power and influence over the state government. Supporters of government reform, known as Progressives, protested the tax breaks and other favors granted to big business by the state legislature. There was little these reformers could do, however, because Pennsylvania's state government was largely controlled by a Republican Party "machine"

As young boys play in the foreground, smoke pours from the chimneys of Pittsburgh's Homestead steel plant in this 1903 photograph. A few years after this picture was taken, Pittsburgh's population passed the half-million mark.

headed by Boies Penrose, one of the legendary political bosses of the era.

Pennsylvania's industrial muscle was again put to the test when the United States entered World War I in 1917. Some 3,000 businesses—from huge steel plants to small shops—turned out products for the war effort. The state made an especially important contribution in shipbuilding: The Hog Island shipyards, in the Delaware River, launched scores of destroyers for the U.S. Navy, plus hundreds of merchant ships.

In the 1920s, Pennsylvania's government finally went through a period of reform under the governorship of Gifford Pinchot (1923–27 and 1931–35). Pinchot, who had earlier helped Theodore Roosevelt set up the U.S. Forest Service, also made conservation of the state's natural resources an important goal. During his first term in office, 500,000 acres of forest were set aside as public land, and the

The American International Shipbuilding Corporation's Hog Island shipyard was hailed as a model of efficiency during World War I. Using assembly line production methods, cargo ships like the one under construction in this photograph (top) were completed in record time.

Connecticut-born Gifford Pinchot (right) first entered Pennsylvania politics as an unsuccessful candidate for the U.S. Senate in 1914. As Pennsylvania's commissioner of forestry (1920–22), however, Pinchot challenged party "bosses" for control of the state's Republican organization, and his victory in this political battle helped him win the governorship in 1922.

Grimed with coal dust, an anthracite miner drills coal in a mine near Scranton in this 1930s photograph. This miner was lucky to have a job; between 1930 and 1932 alone, coal production in Pennsylvania fell by 20 million tons, throwing many miners out of work.

state government carried out an ambitious program aimed at cleaning up waterways that had been polluted by decades of industrial growth.

Pinchot returned for a second term in 1931. By this time, Pennsylvania was in the depths of the terrible economic depression that began with the Stock Market Crash of 1929. The depression led to the closing of 4,000 coal mines, and in one year (1933) half of all the state's steel workers were laid off. In the heavily industrialized region around Pittsburgh, as many as four out of five workers were without a job; hunger, homelessness, and misery spread throughout the state.

The state government responded by passing the 1932 Talbot Act, which provided aid to the jobless, and Pennsylvania received much help from the federal government in the form of President Franklin Roosevelt's New Deal programs.

The state also set up its own public works program to put some of the unemployed back to work. The chief accomplishment of this "Little New Deal," as some called it, was the building of the Pennsylvania Turnpike, the first multi-lane highway in the country. Work began in 1938, and the first section of the turnpike, between Carlisle and Irwin, opened to motorists in 1940.

Still, the state's slumping economy didn't spring back to life until World War II, when orders for defense products came flooding in. During the war years, Pennsylvania ranked second in the nation in the production of goods for the war effort. The state provided one-third of the coal and steel and one-fourth of all the ships used by the United States in the war.

Pennsylvania's human contribution in World War II was no less impressive. About 1.2 million men and women from the state—more than 10 percent of Pennsylvania's adult population—served in the armed forces during the conflict. About 33,000 lost their lives before the war ended in August 1945.

Molten steel is tipped into a blast furnace at a Pittsburgh plant in 1942 (top). Pennsylvania provided almost a third of the steel used by the Allied forces in World War II.

With many male workers fighting overseas, Pennsylvania's women took their places in plants, mills, and factories across the state. Here (right), a woman worker cleans out a grinding machine in a metal shop.

Pennsylvania Since World War II

In the decades following World War II, Pennsylvania's population growth, which had risen steadily for more than a century, began to slow. The Census of 1950 (which counted about 10.5 million Pennsylvanians) also showed that the state had dropped to third place in population among the states. By 1980, Pennsylvania had fallen to fourth place, and to fifth in 1990.

The great era of immigration ended around World War I. At the beginning of the 20th century, Pennsylvania had the second-highest percentage of foreign-born citizens among the states. By 1980, the reverse was true; Pennsylvania had the highest percentage of native-born citizens in the nation.

The state's population changed in makeup as well as in number. During both world wars, large numbers of African Americans moved to Pennsylvania from the rural South to work in the state's defense industries. Most settled in urban areas.

In 1946, two engineers, John Mauchly and J. Presper Eckert, Jr., designed the first modern, general-purpose electronic computer, which went into service at the University of Pennsylvania. Called ENIAC—short for Electronic Numerical Integrator and Calculator—the computer weighed more than thirty tons and used 500 miles of wiring.

Pennsylvania was generally prosperous from the 1940s through the early 1960s, when the "big three" industries—raw materials, metals, and manufacturing—began declining. Texas and other states had already replaced Pennsylvania as the nation's leading oil producer, while the shift from coal to oil as a heating and industrial fuel hurt the state's coal mines. Factory output fell as manufacturing became less important to the nation's economy.

No industry was harder hit than Pittsburgh's steel mills. Starting in the early 1960s, businesses began to buy cheaper steel from overseas. As a result, plants began to lay off workers and shut their doors. Some steel-producing towns lost one-third of their jobs during the 1970s.

This slowdown was keenly felt in the state's poorer areas, especially the African-American neighborhoods of Philadelphia, where economic problems fueled racial tensions. In 1964, these tensions boiled over into three days of rioting, in which about 500 people were injured.

On March 28, 1979, the nuclear power plant at Three Mile Island suffered a serious accident, releasing clouds of radioactive steam across the Susquehanna River Valley. Luckily, technicians brought the plant under control before radiation hit deadly levels, but the accident—the most serious ever to hit a nuclear plant in the United States—left Pennsylvania with a difficult and expensive cleanup job.

The nation's first commercial nuclear power plant opened at Shippingport, Pennsylvania, in 1957; twenty-two years later, however, a serious accident at the Three Mile Island nuclear plant led many Pennsylvanians to wonder if nuclear energy was worth the risks involved. Here (right), a woman protests at the state capital in the aftermath of the Three Mile Island accident.

Developed by American engineers at the University of Pennsylvania in 1946, this thirty-ton computer (below), called ENIAC, began operation as the world's first practical digital computer. Slow and extremely large by today's standards—it used 18,000 vacuum tubes for its calculations—ENIAC was nonetheless a major landmark in the development of computers.

The Keystone State Today

Like many states, Pennsylvania has worked hard to maintain a balance that both encourages modern change and protects its rich historical roots.

Not far from Philadelphia is Lancaster County, home to much of Pennsylvania's Amish community. The Amish continue to live as they have for more than two hundred years, favoring horses and buggies over cars and living without electricity and telephones. Even without modern conveniences, however, Amish farms are among the most productive in the nation.

Amish children draw water from a hand-pumped well in Lancaster County. While farming is the traditional occupation of the Amish, today many people are involved in trades that will directly benefit the community, such as carpentry, shoemaking, and beekeeping.

Yet Pennsylvania of the 1980s and 1990s is also the story of a state coping with change. Throughout the last decade and a half, Pennsylvania's government and people have done much to solve the problems of the present and prepare for the future.

For example, Pennsylvania has replaced some of the jobs lost in the old "smokestack industries" with new jobs in service industries, especially tourism. With its great natural beauty and wealth of cultural and historical sites, Pennsylvania is growing in popularity as a destination for tourists and vacationers. Today, tourism employs as many Pennsylvanians as the steel plants did a few decades ago.

Recent years have also seen the rise of "high-tech" industries—computer components, electronics, and telecommunications—in the state.

Both Philadelphia and Pittsburgh have completed ambitious programs of urban renewal aimed at reviving their downtown areas. Pittsburgh's revival centered on the rebuilding of the city's decayed Golden Triangle, the point where the Ohio, Monongahela, and Allegheny rivers meet. Pittsburgh's rebirth was a great success: In the late 1980s, *The Places Rated Almanac* named it the best major American city to live in.

Still, problems of unemployment, high crime, education, and poor housing continue to trouble Pennsylvania's urban areas, especially Philadelphia.

In 1984, the city, now 40 percent African American, elected its first African-American mayor, Wilson Goode. His election brought a new sense of hope to many Philadelphians.

More than three centuries have passed since William Penn's ship, the *Welcome*, dropped anchor in the Delaware River. Few places in America have witnessed the changes that Pennsylvania has undergone since then, and few places anywhere have experienced so many important events

With its marvelous architecture and wealth of museums and other cultural riches, Pittsburgh has made a remarkable recovery from decades of decline and decay.

on their soil—from the signing of the Declaration of Independence, to the great waves of industrialization and immigration in the 19th century, to the emergence of the modern state. All these have given Pennsylvania a proud and unique history that will endure far into the future.

In the words of the poet Rudyard Kipling: "The things that truly last, when men and time have passed, They are all in Pennsylvania this morning."

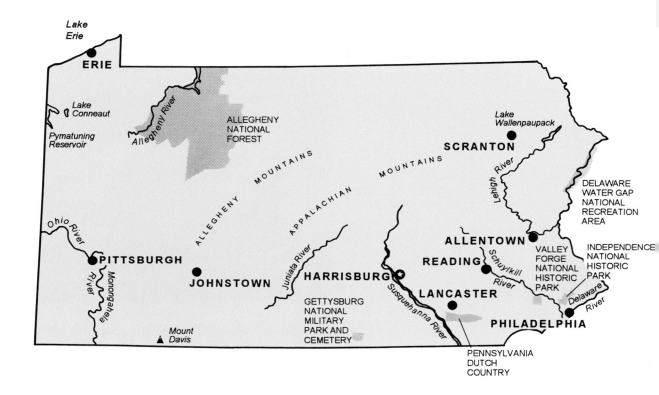

Land area:
> 46,308 square miles, of which 367 are inland water. Ranks 33rd in size.

Major rivers:
> The Allegheny; the Delaware; the Juniata; the Lehigh; the Monongahela; the Ohio; the Schuylkill; the Susquehanna.

Highest point:
> Mount Davis, 3,213 ft.

Major bodies of water:
> Lake Conneaut; Pymatuning Reservoir; Lake Wallenpaupack; and about 300 other lakes and reservoirs. Pennsylvania also has about 50 miles of coastline on Lake Erie.

Climate:
> Average January temperature: 29°F
> Average July temperature: 74°F

Population: 12,050,000 (1993)
Rank: 5th
   1900: 8,720,017
   1790: 434,000

Population of major cities (1992):
Philadelphia	1,585,577
Pittsburgh	369,879
Erie	108,718
Allentown	105,301
Scranton	81,805
Reading	78,380

Ethnic breakdown by percentage (1993):
White	88.0%
African American	9.0%
Hispanic	2.0%
Asian	1.1%
Native American	0.1%

Economy:
Manufacturing (processed foods, machinery, petroleum products, electrical equipment); printing and publishing; tourism; and agriculture (dairy products, grains, vegetables, fruits).

State government:
Legislature: The 2-house legislature consists of a 50-member senate and a 203-member house of representatives. Senators serve for 4 years, representatives for 2 years.
Governor: A governor is elected every 4 years to head the executive branch and is limited to 2 consecutive terms.
Courts: The state's highest court is a 7-justice supreme court. Other courts include a superior court and commonwealth court.
State capital: Harrisburg

State Flag

The state flag consists of a blue background and Pennsylvania's coat-of-arms, which includes a ship, a plow, and grain, symbolizing industry and agriculture; an eagle, symbolizing bravery; and an olive branch, symbolizing peace. The flag was adopted in 1907.

State Seal

The front of the seal includes the state's coat of arms; on the reverse is a figure of a woman, representing liberty, standing over a defeated lion, who represents tyranny. Above the figures are the words "Both can't survive."

State Motto

"Virtue, Liberty, and Independence."

State Nickname

The "Keystone State," from its location at the center of the thirteen original states. Pennsylvania is also known as the "Quaker State," from the religious group that played a large part in its founding.

Places to See

Carnegie Museum of Art, Pittsburgh

Delaware Water Gap National Recreation Area, Bushkill

Drake Well Museum, Titusville

Eisenhower National Historic Site, Gettysburg

Flagship Niagara Reconstruction, Erie

Fort Necessity National Battlefield, Uniontown

Franklin Institute, Philadelphia

Gettysburg National Military Park, Gettysburg

Hershey Chocolate Plant and Hersheypark, Hershey

Hopewell Furnace National Historic Site, Birdsboro

Independence National Historical Park, Philadelphia

Johnstown Flood National Memorial, St. Michael

Little League Museum, Williamsport

Museum of Anthracite Mining, Ashland

Pennsylvania Dutch Country, Berks, Lancaster, and York counties

Philadelphia Museum of Art, Philadelphia

Philadelphia Zoo, Philadelphia

State Museum, Harrisburg

Steamtown National Historic Site, Scranton

Valley Forge National Historic Park, Valley Forge

State Song

Pennsylvania, Pennsylvania
Mighty is your name
Steeped in glory and tradition
Object of acclaim
Where brave men fought the foe of freedom
Tyranny decried
'Til the bell of independence
Filled the countryside
✳

Pennsylvania, Pennsylvania
May your future be filled
With honor everlasting
As your history
✳

Pennsylvania, Pennsylvania
Blessed by God's own hand
Birthplace of a mighty nation
Keystone of the land
Where our first country's flag unfolded
Freedom to proclaim
May the voices of tomorrow
Glorify your name
✳

Pennsylvania, Pennsylvania
May your future be filled
With honor everlasting
As your history

State Flower

Pennnsylvania's state flower is the mountain laurel, an evergreen shrub that can reach thirty feet in height. Its white and rose-colored flowers are a common sight on many of the state's hillsides.

State Bird

A game bird found in Pennsylvania's mountainous areas, the ruffed grouse is Pennsylvania's state bird. The brown-and-tan-feathered bird is a favorite of hunters.

State Tree

The Eastern hemlock is Pennsylvania's state tree. Growing to a height of about sixty feet, the Eastern hemlock has reddish-brown bark and small cones.

Pennsylvania History

1609 Henry Hudson explores Delaware Bay

1638 Swedish colonists found New Sweden on the banks of the Delaware River

1641 Swedes establish a fort on Tinicum Island

1655 Dutch forces take control of New Sweden

1664 Pennsylvania region comes under British rule

1681 King Charles II grants present-day Pennsylvania to William Penn

1682 Penn founds the city of Philadelphia

1683 Religious refugees from Germany found Germantown

1704 Lower counties on the Delaware become a separate colony

1723 Benjamin Franklin arrives in Philadelphia from Boston

1751 Dr. Benjamin Rush of Philadelphia founds the first modern hospital in the 13 colonies

1754 Fighting between French troops and British-colonial forces at Fort Necessity sparks the French and Indian War

1768 Pennsylvania Assembly formally protests taxes imposed by the British Parliament

1776 Meeting in Philadelphia, the Second Continental Congress adopts the Declaration of Independence

American

1492 Christopher Columbus reaches the New World

1607 Jamestown (Virginia) founded by English colonists

1620 *Mayflower* arrives at Plymouth (Massachusetts)

1754–63 French and Indian War

1765 Parliament passes Stamp Act

1775–83 Revolutionary War

1776 Signing of the Declaration of Independence

1788–90 First congressional elections

1791 Bill of Rights added to U.S. Constitution

1803 Louisiana Purchase

1812–14 War of 1812

1820 Missouri Compromise

1836 Battle of the Alamo, Texas

1846–48 Mexican-American War

1849 California Gold Rush

1860 South Carolina secedes from Union

1861–65 Civil War

1862 Lincoln signs Homestead Act

1863 Emancipation Proclamation

1865 President Lincoln assassinated (April 14)

1865–77 Reconstruction in the South

1866 Civil Rights bill passed

1881 President James Garfield shot (July 2)

History

1896 First Ford automobile is made

1898–99 Spanish-American War

1901 President William McKinley is shot (Sept. 6)

1917 U.S. enters World War I

1922 Nineteenth Amendment passed, giving women the vote

1929 U.S. stock market crash; Great Depression begins

1933 Franklin D. Roosevelt becomes president; begins New Deal

1941 Japanese attack Pearl Harbor (Dec. 7); U.S. enters World War II

1945 U.S. drops atomic bomb on Hiroshima and Nagasaki; Japan surrenders, ending World War II

1963 President Kennedy assassinated (November 22)

1964 Civil Rights Act passed

1965–73 Vietnam War

1968 Martin Luther King, Jr., shot in Memphis (April 4)

1974 President Richard Nixon resigns because of Watergate scandal

1979–81 Hostage crisis in Iran: 52 Americans held captive for 444 days

1989 End of U.S.-Soviet cold war

1991 Gulf War

1993 U.S. signs North American Free Trade Agreement with Canada and Mexico

Pennsylvania History

1780 Pennsylvania abolishes slavery within its borders

1787 Constitutional Convention meets in Philadelphia • Pennsylvania becomes the second state to ratify the Constitution

1790-1800 Philadelphia serves as the capital of the United States

1794 Whiskey Rebellion in western Pennsylvania as farmers protest federal taxes

1856 James Buchanan, born in Mercersburg, is elected president

1859 Edwin Drake drills the first successful American oil well near Titusville

1863 Union forces defeat Confederates at Gettysburg in the turning point of the Civil War

1889 More than 2,000 people die in the Johnstown Flood

1920 KDKA in Pittsburgh is the first commercial radio station in the U.S.

1940 First major section of the Pennsylvania Turnpike is opened to traffic

1979 Accident at Three Mile Island nuclear power plant raises fears about the use of atomic energy

1984 W. Wilson Goode wins election as Philadelphia's first black mayor

1988 Tank spill in Pittsburgh dumps 1 million gallons of oil into the Monongahela and Ohio rivers

William Penn (1664–1718)

The son of an admiral in the Royal Navy, Penn became a Quaker and founded Pennsylvania with a grant of land from King Charles II. Penn is remembered as one of the most enlightened colonial leaders, both for his belief in religious tolerance and his insistence on fair treatment for the Native Americans.

John Bartram (1699–1777)

A native of Chester County, the "Father of American Botany" was among the first scientists to study North American plant life.

Benjamin Franklin (1706–90)

One of the leading figures in colonial America, Franklin (a Philadelphian from 1723) was a printer, writer, scientist, diplomat, inventor, and politician.

Benjamin West (1738–1820)

Born in Philadelphia, West was one of the first American artists to gain an international reputation.

Benjamin Rush (1746–1813)

This Philadelphian was both a Patriot leader (he signed the Declaration of Independence) and an innovative doctor whose ideas about addiction, mental illness, and hygiene were far ahead of his time.

James Buchanan (1791–1868)

Born in Mercersburg, Buchanan was a representative, senator, secretary of state, and diplomat before winning the presidency as a Democrat in the election of 1856.

Thaddeus Stevens (1792–68)

Stevens was an outspoken opponent of slavery and promoter of racial equality. As a "Radical Republican" U.S. representative from Philadelphia, he led the move to impose harsh Reconstruction policies on the defeated Confederacy.

Lucretia Coffin Mott (1793–1880)

Born in Massachusetts, this Quaker leader moved to Philadelphia in 1809. Her long life was spent fighting against slavery and for women's rights.

Andrew Carnegie (1835–1919)

This Scotland-born industrialist founded Carnegie Steel Company, Pittsburgh's greatest steel producer. Much of his vast fortune went toward founding

Mary Cassatt

libraries, museums, and foundations.

Mary Cassatt (1847–1926)

Considered by many to be America's greatest woman painter, Cassatt, who was born in Allegheny City, produced many masterpieces in the Impressionist style.

Andrew William Mellon (1855–1937)

Born into Pittsburgh's important Mellon family, Andrew served as secretary of the treasury from 1921 to 1932. A great art collector, he founded the Mellon Institute in Pittsburgh and the National Gallery of Art in Washington, D.C.

Gifford Pinchot (1865–1946)

As chief of the U.S. Forest Service, Pinchot

was an important ally of President Theodore Roosevelt in the movement to conserve America's natural resources. He later served two terms as governor of Pennsylvania.

George Catlett Marshall (1880–1959) Born in Uniontown, Marshall's brilliant military career was capped by service as the U.S. Army's chief of staff during World War II. After the war, he served as both secretary of state and secretary of defense.

Martha Graham (1894–1994) Born in Allegheny, Graham was one of the most influential modern dance performers and teachers of the 20th century.

Alexander Calder (1898–1976) This artist is best known for his free-moving sculptures. His father, Alexander Milne Calder, sculpted the figure of William Penn that tops Philadelphia's city hall.

Margaret Mead (1901–78) *Coming of Age in Samoa* (1928) established this Philadelphia native as one of America's most important anthropologists. She also pioneered the use of photography and film in recording the customs and rituals of primitive societies.

Marian Anderson

Marian Anderson (1902–93) Born in Philadelphia, Anderson, who began singing in church choirs, became one of the most renowned musical voices of the 20th century.

B. F. Skinner (1904–90) A psychologist best known for his research into how people learn and behave, Skinner, a Susquehanna native, popularized his ideas in books like *Walden Two* and *Beyond Freedom and Dignity.*

Rachel Carson (1907–64) A pioneer of the environmental movement, this native of Springdale is best known for her book *Silent Spring*, a warning about the dangers of chemical pesticides on natural habitats.

Samuel Barber (1910–81) Two-time winner of the Pulitzer Prize for music, this native of West Chester is one of the most important 20th-century American composers.

Andrew Wyeth (b. 1917) Born in Chadds Ford, artist Andrew Wyeth is known for precise yet mysterious paintings like *Christina's World.*

Andy Warhol (1928–87) Warhol left Pittsburgh for New York City in 1949. Winning fame for his "pop art" paintings in the 1960s, he became one of the most influential and controversial artists of the 20th century.

John Updike (b. 1932) A winner of the Pulitzer Prize, this Shillington-born poet, essayist, and novelist has touched on Pennsylvania life in many of his books.

Wilton "Wilt" Chamberlain (b. 1936) The holder of many professional basketball records, Chamberlain spent much of his fourteen-year professional career playing in his native Philadelphia.

Pictures in this volume:

American Swedish Historical Museum, Philadelphia, Pennsylvania: 12-13

Abby Aldrich Rockefeller Folk Art Center, Williamsburg, VA: 18

Dover: 14, 26 (top), 26 (bottom), 39, 45, 47 (bottom)

Library of Congress: 7, 9, 10, 13, 14, 15 (top), 15 (bottom), 16, 17, 19, 20 (top), 20 (bottom), 22, 24-25, 28, 29, 30, 31, 34, 38-39, 40, 41, 42, 43, 44, 46, 49 (bottom), 61

National Archives: 49 (top), 51 (top)

Pennsylvania Dutch Convention and Visitors Bureau: 52

Pennsylvania Office of Travel Marketing: 53

Pennsylvania State Archives: 35, 47 (top), 48

Pennsylvania Tourism Bureau: 2

The State Museum of Pennsylvania, Pennsylvania Historical and Museum Commission: 33

University of Pennsylvania Archives: 51 (bottom)

About the author:

Charles A. Wills is a writer, editor, and consultant specializing in American history. He has written, edited, or contributed to more than thirty books, including many volumes in The Millbrook Press's *American Albums from the Collections of the Library of Congress* series. He lives in Dutchess County, New York.

Suggested reading:

Cochran, Thomas Childs, *Pennsylvania: A Bicentennial History*, New York: Norton, 1978

Fradin, Dennis B., *From Sea to Shining Sea: Pennsylvania*, Chicago: Childrens Press, 1994

Kent, Deborah, *America the Beautiful: Pennsylvania*, Chicago: Childrens Press, 1988

Lorwen, Nancy, *Great Cities of the United States: Philadelphia*, Vero Beach, FL: Rourke Enterprises, 1989

Parker, Steve, *Benjamin Franklin*, New York: Chelsea House Publishers, 1995

Peck, Ira, *Pennsylvania: A History of the Keystone State*, New York: Scholastic Inc., 1985

Seitz, Ruth Hoover, *Amish Ways*, Harrisburg, PA: RB Books, 1991

Wild, Terry, *Pennsylvania: A Photographic Celebration*, Helena, MT: American Geographic Publishers, 1989

For more information contact:

Pennsylvania Office of Travel Marketing
453 Forum Building
Harrisburg, PA 17120
Tel. (717) 787-5453

Pennsylvania Historical and Museum Commission
Third and North Street, Box 1026
Harrisburg, PA 17108
Tel. (717) 787-2891

INDEX

Page numbers in *italics* indicate illustrations